Winning Your Battle Against Suicide

Geary Reid

ISBN: 978-976-8305-20-6

Acknowledgements

Great thanks must be expressed to the following people:

The heavenly Father, for granting me the wisdom and inspiration to record the information in this book, which I began on August 8, 2020, and completed on August 16, 2020; my family, for their continued encouragement and support regarding various challenges; and several people who have assisted with reviewing and editing the book:

- Wonnette Nicholson, Dipl. in Business Management and Administration
- Leslyn Harcourt, Bs. Mgmt. Dipl. in Accountancy, Associate Degree in Education
- Shawn Rogers, Adv. Dipl. Project Mgmt., A+ Certification, Telecommunication Certification
- Judah Louisy, MSc, ACCA, FCPA

To you, the reader: have fun while reading, and grasp and practice what you learn so that this world will become a better place. Many people are depending on your guidance. We all need a shoulder to lean on and a hand to guide us.

Geary Reid
MBA, FCCA, FAAPM, MPM, CAT

Reid's Learning Institute and Business Consultancy

reidnlearn.com

Amazon: amazon.com/author/gearyreid

Facebook: Reid n Learn

Instagram: Reid n Learn

LinkedIn: Reid's Learning Institute
and Business Consultancy

199 Kuru - Kururu, Soesdyke Linden Highway
Guyana, South America

Table of Contents

Introduction

Suicide takes life, but today you will win the battle against suicide! Make suicide your enemy.

If you have lost hope or are contemplating suicide, this book urges you not to give up. It is divided into three important sections. It first acknowledges many of the problems that persons face, then provides hope in the second section. Finally, it encourages persons to rejoice, as they have stayed alive and must be considered winners.

You will not find scientific evidence in this book on how to win your battle against suicide. However, you will find many practical things that you can use to win this important battle. You do not have to be an expert to take control of your thoughts. Listen to some motivational songs, and you can probably sing and dance. Find ways to enjoy life. Avoid being depressed. Through this book, you will see that you have many simple ways to stay alive.

Do you know that everyone has problems? Your problems may appear to be like a mountain, but it may be a pebble compared to the problems that other persons face. Do not give up on your dreams. If you can stay alive today, then you can stay alive for tomorrow. Some of your problems have nothing to do with you. Problems can develop as a result of people around us, so it may not be that you have done anything wrong. Even if you did not provide an invitation, problems will still visit you, whether you are poor or rich.

Overcoming problems will require a variety of approaches. Some problems may be overcome using simple things, but others require many complex things to be overcome. If a person is willing to seek help, then they will overcome their problems. Those who do not overcome their problems will soon be overcome by them.

Once you have overcome your problems, congratulations, you are a winner. Be thankful for all those who supported you. Let them know how much you appreciated their support during your time of trouble.

Go to help other persons to overcome their suicidal thoughts. Share with them some of your experiences of how you won this battle against suicide. Everyone is important, so do not let anyone lose their life to suicide. Pray for them and encourage them to make good decisions. There are many good things ahead for the living. Suicide must be viewed as a person's enemy and not their friend. While we face many problems in life, it is better to stay alive than to be dead, as those who are alive have the power to make a positive difference in this world.

Section A: Problems everywhere

A problem is like an uninvited guest. It doesn't only visit the poor, but also the rich. A problem will remain longer with anyone who will not work feverishly to get rid of it.

Under the earth's surface, there are problems. Above the earth, there are problems. Some of the problems that persons encounter started in their childhood days. Those problems are vivid in their minds, and although the problem might have occurred many years ago, it is still fresh in some persons' minds, as if it happened yesterday. Someone who had problems at school may still remember their teacher and the date of the event long after their student years. Parents can also contribute to some children's bad experiences.

Not all relatives are there to help each other. For some persons, the biggest disappointments they experience are with their relatives. Those who live in an extended family will have both good days and bad days. With extended family, everyone has their views and beliefs. Sometimes, each person feels that what they think must be executed in the same manner that they want it to occur.

Those who are working may have enjoyable days, but they may also have some days of regret. For example, poor infrastructure and poor working conditions can add more problems to a person's working life. Some persons may have a boss instead of a leader. The boss is not willing to take any advice but needs things to be done as instructed. Employees who hate to be bossed around will change their position in the organization or may even quit the organization entirely.

Crime is so well known in some communities that when the name of that community is mentioned, the only thoughts that flow through some persons' minds are all the bad things they have heard about it. Persons who live in such communities may be rejected, not because they are uneducated, but because of the stigma attached to the communities from which they hail.

No relationship is perfect. However, some relationships seem to have more problems than you could ever imagine, and not all persons know how to address their relationship issues. Owning a home or a vehicle may also be challenging. Not all financial institutions are willing to assist the poor, and they may demand many requirements. This may result in persons continuing to live in rented places. No government will allow ordinary citizens to own land. There are some landlords who are only interested in the tenants' fee and therefore do not maintain the building regularly.

1. Everyone has problems

Those who are having problems often think that they are the only one, but this is not true. Everyone has problems. However, each person will address their problems differently.

No one is isolated from problems, since problems are everywhere. Some persons make a great effort to stay away from problems, yet problems still find them wherever they go. They may begin to blame themselves and oftentimes think that something went wrong because they were born. They may express their frustration by making evil comments about their birth.

1.1 Problems do not have special friends

Problems never knock at someone's door and, when it sees the occupants, apologize to them because a special friend is living in that house. Many persons would be happy if they could have avoided a problem by establishing a good relationship with it.

To accept the problem as a friend (or as a natural and acceptable thing) is a bad choice for anyone. No one must settle in their minds that they will allow themselves to be overcome by a problem and not continue to fight against it.

1.2 Problems like people

Inanimate things are not affected by problems, but humans are constantly affected by problems. The problems that humans encounter are numerous and will never decrease. While people may take vacations from their work to give themselves some rest, problems never take a vacation.

Figure 1. Problems are constantly searching for people

(All figures developed by the author unless otherwise noted.)

Not many persons are willing to fight against problems. They may even be willing to give in to the problems that confront them.

1.3 Problems do not look for rewards

When a problem visits an individual, it is not looking for rewards. The problem does not have any feelings and therefore is not the least bit interested in how people respond to it. No one has to acknowledge the problem, since they will not be given any respect or acknowledgment.

If every person were to ask another person if they had problems, the answer would always be "Yes." Therefore, it is evident that everyone has problems, but problems must not be embraced. Everyone must fight against the problem, not celebrate it.

2. Problems from childhood days

Persons who go through depression and struggle with negative feelings may remember challenges that started when they were younger. While it is known that problems may occur at any point within someone's life, some persons can trace their problems back to their childhood days.

2.1 Young persons are affected

Depression and suicidal thoughts will affect many persons. Many young persons will often mention that they had suicidal thoughts and some of them found no solutions. Even though the thought may flow through the minds of many persons, they must be willing to resist such thoughts.

2.2 Childhood problems with parents

The relationships between children and their parents can be very challenging. Some children believe incorrectly that they do not have to follow the guidance of their parents. On the other hand, some parents may take the dictatorship approach to the family and even to their children.

When children are young, parents may take some actions on their own; however, as children age, it may be best to engage them in discussions and negotiations. Once children recognize that their voice or views are not being heard and understood, they may start to believe that they do not have any self-worth. Even adults can feel that they do not have any self-worth if their views are not accepted and acted upon. Each human being is entitled to be treated as someone of importance, even though they are not perfect.

Children must be willing to support their parents and learn from them. Even though parents are not perfect humans, children must show them respect, as long as they are not asked to do anything unlawful or unethical.

2.3 Childhood problems with teachers

Not all teachers understand their students. Some students feel that they should be taught even though they do not possess the expected level of knowledge and skills. There is another group of children who feel that they do not have to follow instructions from the teacher and the school.

Students who reject good advice will often hurt their future. Teachers are there to assist students by providing them with education and life-changing experiences. *Students must be willing to learn from their teachers so that their future will be great.*

Teachers possess great knowledge, which will make the students realize their potential. Those students who are willing to follow their teachers find that their learning is enhanced. Resisting teachers' guidance will be harmful to students.

Teachers are not always right. However, students must find different ways to address their concerns while working along with their teachers.

Teachers must maintain a good relationship with the children's parents or guardians to report anything done or perceived about the children. Children need protection and must be seen as important persons.

2.4 Childhood problems with religious leaders

Not all religious leaders may be working in the best interest of the members. Children may not have the ability to make appropriate decisions, so some religious leaders may abuse their privilege of working with them.

Religious leaders are there to help their members. Children must respect and follow the guidance provided to them by their religious leaders.

2.5 Childhood problems with neighbours

Some neighbours are very good for children. They can even be like children's second parents. The relationship may be so good that the parents can ask the neighbours to keep the children for a few hours when there is an urgent matter to address.

In each community, neighbours may vary in their beliefs and how they treat others. Within some rural communities, most neighbours know each other and look out for each other. This may not be the case in urban communities, where persons are often occupied with employment activities and may not have the time to provide any assistance to a neighbour's child.

Some children will recall that their neighbours mistreated them. This negative experience of treatment can cause these children to become depressed.

Parents must have an open approach with their children and be willing to listen to them. They must not ignore them, since those children may be looking for a trusted adult they can share their concerns with.

2.6 Childhood problems with relatives

Though many relatives are helpful to the children in their families, some will mistreat children. The pain that those children go through remains with them for a long time. Those bad memories live on with those children and may even plague their minds when they are adults.

3. Problems in your relationship

Relationships are good. Persons get connected with their partners for many reasons that may keep them together for many years. Falling in love with someone for the first time often feels exciting, but keeping the relationship alive may be a challenge. Some persons fall in love and marry, while others may decide to have a common-law relationship.

Everyone is trying to build a strong relationship, but no relationship is free from problems, regardless of the length of time persons may be living together.

Figure 2. Each relationship will have mountain and valley experiences

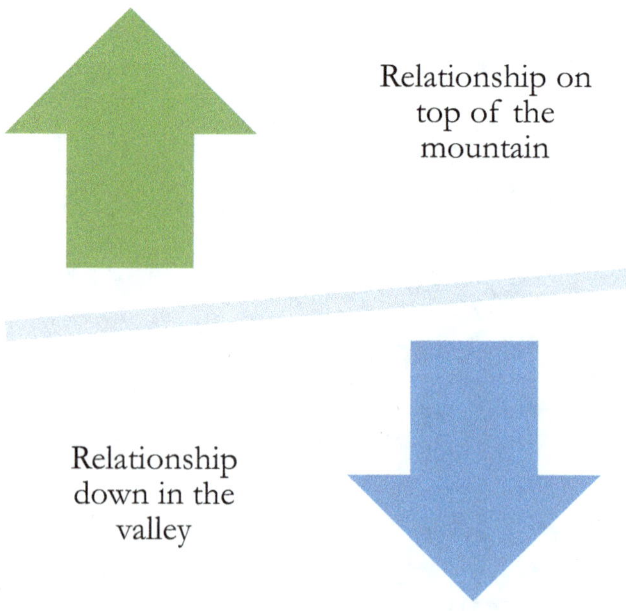

3.1 Building relationships takes time

Every relationship takes time to build. It is not something that will happen within a second. Many couples will indicate the number of years that they have been in a relationship and the challenges that they are still going through.

Each person in a relationship has their own likes and dislikes, along with their own views and beliefs. They may often try to get the other person to become like their child, but not everyone will accept that approach. Each person must be given autonomy to operate within the relationship, but to build the relationship that they are already in.

3.2 Disagreement is a part of relationships

Disagreement is a part of every relationship, as both persons will not always see the same thing in the same manner. Disagreement is not a bad thing, but it is important to find a way for each person to be able to maintain their view on a particular matter without disrespecting the other person. Respect must be shown to those who have different views.

To help embrace each other, there will be a need to have both persons get to know each other more and for them to find more common ground to agree on some matters. Too often, if both parties have multiple disagreements, those disagreements will lead to numerous problems in the relationship. and then both persons will begin to have a different feeling for the person they once loved.

3.3 Living as enemies is unacceptable

Those who are in relationships must not live as enemies. They must be able to move beyond their disagreement and reconcile. Every relationship will find challenging moments, but there is a need to push beyond those challenges and remember why both persons came together.

Some persons do not think that it is important to forgive, and so they see their partner as their biggest stumbling block. A person's real enemy is not their partner, so they need to stop seeing and treating their partner as an enemy.

As long as one partner holds envious feelings in his or her mind towards the other partner, the relationship will not progress. This has been a major challenge for many persons, which causes partners to become frustrated.

Forgiveness is available to everyone, but not everyone is willing to allow forgiveness to flow in their relationships. Healing can occur in any troubled relationship, but both persons must be prepared to cooperate.

When relationships go through challenging moments, especially for a prolonged period, one of the partners may try to distance him or herself from the other. This can add more frustration to the other partner and make the relationship uncomfortable.

If one member of the relationship continues to feel belittled, then they may look at ways to exit the relationship. While there may be many ways to heal the relationship, some persons become adamant that they no longer want to be a part of it.

Each person must be careful of the words that they utter. Once words are released, they go towards their assignment without any further instructions. So, each partner must be careful about what they say.

Angry persons must refrain from doing things that will harm their partner or the relationship. Both verbal and nonverbal communication, if not properly done, can harm the relationship.

4. Problems at your workplace

Places of employment are often wonderful, and persons have many reasons why they work. Some choose to work so that they will earn for themselves, while others may choose to work because they want to keep themselves occupied. Some will choose to work because their home is a place where there are many problems, and when they attend work, they find some comfort.

When the workplace becomes a challenge, many employees will become frustrated and probably want to change workplaces. Not all employees can continue working in a place where they do not feel comfortable or their voice is not heard.

4.1 Boss instead of a leader

Most organizations employ persons who meet the required age to work, and therefore, those persons must be respected as adults. Each employee must have a sense that they have equal entitlement to the standard service that the organization offers. They want to know that they can respectfully share their views at the appropriate time and that someone listens to them.

But those who are placed to provide supervision can sometimes become a dictator at the workplace. Oftentimes, those supervisors who operate as bosses do not want to take suggestions from subordinates and will only want the work to be done according to their instruction, even if their guidance is incorrect. Supervisors must be caring individuals who will allow employees to know that they have a friend and confidant.

Figure 3. The boss drives employees away and the leader retains employees

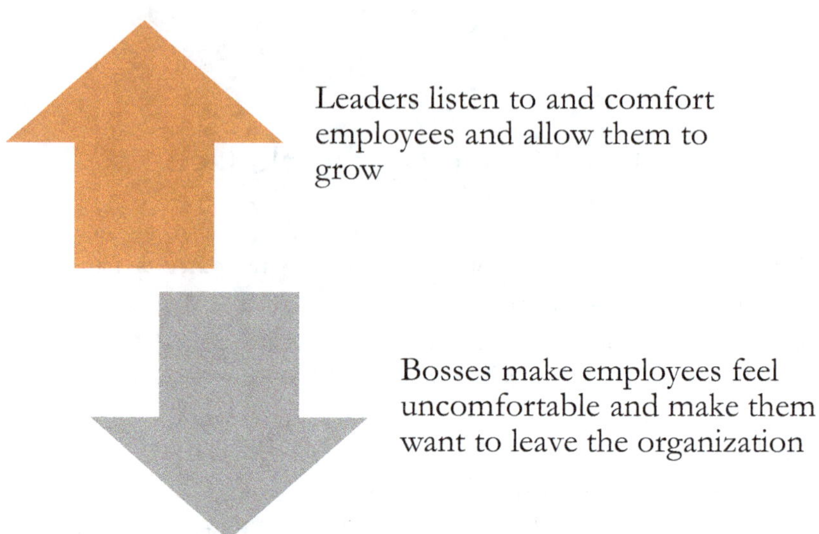

Not all homes are a safe place for every member of the family, and if employees have problems at home or with their companions, they do not want to be at work and feel the same pressures of life.

If the leader takes some time to assess the employees' situation, some employees will be open to discussing important matters that will help the leader to have a better understanding of the employee. There must a relationship between supervisors and their subordinates.

There need to be fewer bosses and more leaders in the workplace. Bosses drive employees away from organizations, while leaders cause employees to see their true potential and make the organization their second home.

When employees feel that they are oppressed because of bosses, they will often seek opportunities to quit their employment, especially, if no one listens to their genuine concerns. Many organizations continue to lose quality employees because some supervisors do not care about the employee, but only care about themselves and production.

Every human being must be respected. Their age or status must never be the deciding factor for respecting them.

4.2 Poor working conditions

The organization may have leaders whose employees are comfortable with the working conditions even though they may be unacceptable or unsuitable for humans and even animals. Employees should be aware that their health and safety are important to them and should be to their employers as well.

Poor working conditions, which can lead to accidents and incidents in the workplace, have caused many organizations to be sued. While employee negligence is another reason for accidents and incidents, employers must at least provide proper working conditions for employees.

Figure 4. Working conditions lead employees to stay or leave the organization

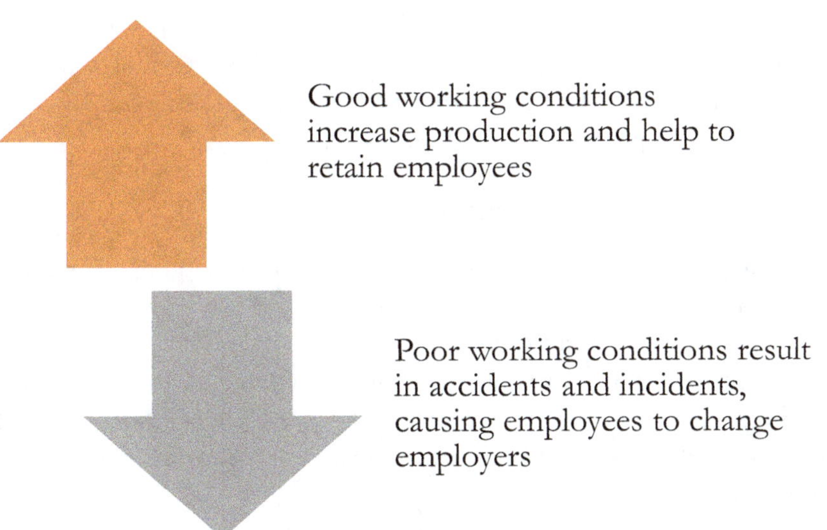

While the compensation may be attractive, employees may choose to leave the organization, since their health and well-being must not be compromised. Employers, money may not be able to restore your employees' lives, so protect them first.

4.3 Poor infrastructure

In some workplaces, the infrastructure is poor. Employees complain to management, but to no avail.

Poor working infrastructure makes employees frustrated, and a frustrated employee will be less productive for the employer. Management needs to create an environment where employees can share their concerns. Those concerns shared by employees must be acted upon by management in a timely manner. Management may not be able to fix every matter immediately, but they should communicate with employees and indicate their intent to fix the matter.

A frustrated employee can be dangerous to him or herself and to the organization. Frustrated employees look for any opportunity to relieve their frustration, and they do not consider the consequences of their actions. The only thing that they may be thinking of is finding a way out of their frustration, even if it will cost them their life.

Some employers have counsellors in the workplace to listen to and help employees. Human Resource departments are expected to listen to their employees' concerns and provide appropriate solutions. If some of the solutions are not within the organization's capabilities, then external assistance must be sought, but the employee must not be left to provide their own solution to a problem that is all work-related.

4.4 Inadequate compensation

No employer can always provide all of the compensation that employees demand. The needs of employees are often great, and they sometimes believe that their employer has all the money they need.

Employers must not withhold that which they can easily provide to their employees. If they are unable to provide adequate compensation, especially for a prolonged period, they must provide an adequate and timely explanation to employees.

All employees have their own set of expenditures, which are separate from their employer's concerns. However, when employees know that their employers can improve their compensation but refuse to do so, then the employees will take actions that are often not in the best interest of the organization. Industrial actions are very evident when employees need increases in compensation, but the employers refuse to adequately compensate them or to keep them informed of the financial status of the organization.

Employers have a responsibility to keep employees informed. While employees will not be provided with information about the entire operation of the organization, some information must be provided to them promptly, without the employees having to demand such information.

Regular meetings with employees are often expected from management. While management may not be able to provide all the answers employees need, they must create a forum to allow employees to share their views about issues such as compensation. If employees are kept informed of the organization's financial status, then they may work towards helping the organization to improve production and revenue.

5. Problems in your community

Every community has its problems. In some communities, there is the problem of high unemployment; in others, it may be gang-related crimes.

So far, no community is perfect. Therefore, everyone must live within their community and make the best use of it.

5.1 Gang-related crimes

When the names of some communities are mentioned, persons can only associate them with gang-related crimes. This situation may have been going on for a long time. This kind of behaviour can often place persons in an uncomfortable position, where they do not have hope in the future, they are frustrated, and they probably think that someday, they may be caught in violence within their community.

While the law enforcement agencies and representatives will make their best effort to provide peace to those communities, persons are often looking for opportunities to harm each other. They wait for any opportunity when the law enforcement officers are not there, and then they create harm and havoc. Many families are disturbed through these activities. Children will often suffer from gang-related incidents. They sometimes lose members of their family, such as their parents or a sibling. Even when the perpetrator is identified, persons are afraid to provide evidence, since their lives may be threatened. Therefore, they are unable and unwilling to report the matter to the legal authorities.

Gang-related violence is always dangerous to any community. It causes more hurts than healing among people.

5.2 Illegal substances

Another issue that plagues some communities is the use and peddling of illegal substances. Both young and old persons within the community may be using those substances.

Many parents will try to guide their children to do the correct things, but some children are influenced by what they see and hear happening within their communities. There are some influential persons within the community who will introduce youths to illegal substances, well knowing the harm it will have upon those children's lives, but they are only interested in getting their product sold.

Many homes and families are fragmented or destroyed because of the use of illegal substances. Illegal substances do not build families but destroy them. Persons' careers have changed because they were servants to illegal substances instead of being the master over them.

5.3 High alcohol consumption

Some homes are destroyed because one person within the home could not control their use of alcohol and began to spend most of their money on it. They often consume amounts that make them intoxicated, and their behaviours become unacceptable while under the influence of alcohol.

Family members of those who consume alcohol are abused and sometimes traumatized. Children sometimes have to seek refuge with other families and in the homes of strangers to survive.

Sadly, sometimes, both parents are engaged in heated exchanges of words. They may even go beyond arguments and become physical, which may cause much harm to one of the parents.

5.4 Domestic violence

In some communities, there is high domestic violence affecting the children and partners of the abusive persons.

While one person may win the argument, many lives are negatively impacted. Some children have seen much domestic violence, which often dissuades them from entering into any relationship. They may also show some negative signs at school or to persons in their communities.

Those who experience domestic violence often look for a way out of the relationship. However, they sometimes fail to take rational steps when making their decision. After they make their decision, many persons regret it, but that was their way of finding an exit to their problems.

Counsellors may be able to provide some assistance, but if their system of obtaining justice is too slow, persons may take the actions that are most comfortable for them. Some family members may be available to provide advice, but on the other hand, some of them may contribute to the domestic issue.

Figure 5. Domestic violence impacts us physically and emotionally

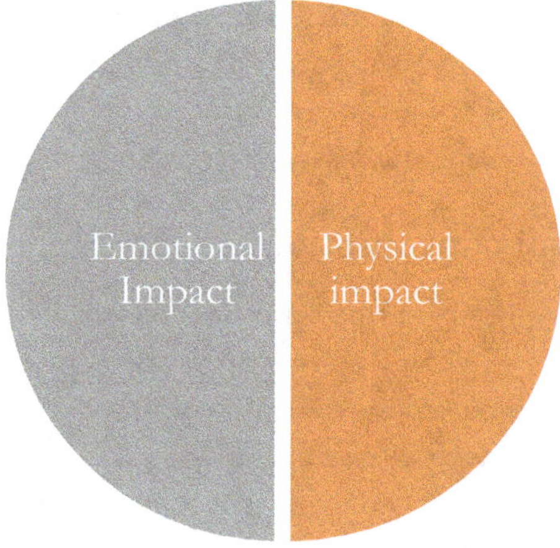

The physical impact of domestic violence may change a person forever. Even a single incident can create much harm that doctors are unable to rectify.

The emotional impact can be with a person for the rest of their life. Some persons become so timid that they feel uncomfortable making basic decisions, since their partner makes them feel that they are unable to make any decision without them. They operate almost like robots and slaves. All of their self-worth is gone, and they often second-guess themselves.

The oppressor in the relationship often feels like a champion, but without recognizing that many lives are impacted and some of this impact will pass from one generation to the next. Some children who witness domestic violence may choose not to find a partner or may treat themselves as someone who does not have value.

5.5 High unemployment

No government can assure all persons that they will provide employment for everyone. Especially in countries with a large population, some persons will have to create their own employment.

The private sector may be a good alternative in the creation of employment. Some individuals must also think about becoming entrepreneurs.

With high unemployment, families can become frustrated and make poor decisions. High unemployment is a recipe for poverty. Those who live in poverty will live lives that are sometimes harmful to themselves and to many others.

Governments sometimes offer social assistance to unemployed persons, but it may not be sufficient for families, especially those with many children. Therefore, more problems are added within the home and some persons are unable to think of appropriate solutions to their problems.

There are some persons who hate to work. They often seek handouts from the government and from anywhere else they can find.

6. Problems with relatives

Some relatives will only be there for you when they need something. When you need their assistance, they are never there. Because not all relatives will be there when you need them, you also need to establish many friends.

There are several family types. These family types are discussed in the table below.

Table 1. Family types

Types of family	Explanation
Nuclear family	The nuclear family consists of a mother, a father, and their children living under the same roof. The nuclear family is common in modern industrial societies.
Single-parent family	As the name itself suggests, the single-parent family consists of only one parent living with his/her child or children.
Sibling family	A family where siblings live together with no parents.
Extended family	As the name itself suggests, the extended family consists of members that extend beyond a mother, a father, and their children.
Reorganized family	A reorganized family is formed when one spouse had an earlier relationship. A previous union may

> have been broken through the death of a spouse or divorce.
>
> One or both spouses may bring a child or children from a former relationship into the new family. In such a family, children may have several stepsisters and stepbrothers.

(Extracted from Ramsawak and Umraw, 2001)

Not everyone feels comfortable living with relatives. Some relatives are only concerned about themselves and do not want anyone to join their family.

6.1 Living with in-laws

When some persons marry, they may choose to live with one partner's parents. The decision to live with in-laws can be a temporary arrangement, but it often lasts longer than initially discussed.

Figure 6. Possible reasons to live with in-laws

- Unable to construct personal property
- Unable to pay lease or rental
- Employment opportunities are only available within the in-laws' community
- No responsible person to provide care for small children
- No personal vehicle or public transportation to transport persons to school and work
- Education facilities are only available within certain catchment areas
- In-laws have a large property and need persons to be there for them
- In-laws may be ill and need someone to assist them when the need arises
- In-laws have physical challenges and must have someone to care for them

The reasons provided above will be common in some families. However, every family living with in-laws has their own reasons for making this arrangement. For example, when some persons marry or choose to establish a common-law relationship, they may not have all of the financial resources needed, so they may find it feasible to live with their in-laws until they can afford certain essential things.

Even though the relationship may start very well, it may not continue in that way, since not all in-laws are comfortable to live with. Some persons complain that at the beginning, they enjoyed a mutual relationship, but it became less and less enjoyable over time, without any major issue being identified.

For example, if the new family who joined the other relatives shows signs of prosperity and progress, it may anger other family members who were not able to make the same progress. Not everyone can be comfortable seeing others prospering, and that may start conflicts among the in-laws.

6.2 Living with extended family

Sometimes, persons may allow other family members to come and live with them. In some communities, parents who are aged may move in to live with their children. Also, if one parent dies, then the other parent may decide to live with one of their children.

Some children may choose to live with their parents after reaching the age of adulthood. They may raise their own family while living with their parents. Grandparents can also benefit from living with their grandchildren. As a matter of fact, some grandchildren will request that their grandparents live with them.

However, as more persons are added to the family, each person may have their personal preferences. The size of the property may not be able to accommodate everyone. With new members added to the family, conflicts may arise, and it may not be possible for anyone in that extended family to resolve those conflicts.

Family conflicts can be numerous and very complex, with no possible short-term solutions. For example, there may be issues with sibling rivalry. This sometimes happens if a parent leaves an asset for the children, but each person cannot find ways to benefit from the same asset. Some of these family matters are eventually solved in the courts, which is a very sad way of resolving a conflict, but it may be the only option that both parties are willing to accept.

6.3 Living in a reorganized family

When both parents have children from previous relationships, it becomes challenging, because some children do not accept the other children into the home. Some children are so protective that they may not want their father or mother to remarry. Therefore, whoever joins the relationship will have to build a good relationship with the children.

The children may not be easy to get along with, especially if they are very suspicious of any new family member. Also, in the reorganized family, the children from both relationships will have different age ranges and will have their own preferences for food, relaxation, and clothing.

Oftentimes, the older children in a reorganized family will try to dictate how the younger children must operate. This approach can create a problem with one of the parents.

The previous lifestyle of some children may not allow them to live peaceably with other families. For example, some children were not accustomed to doing anything at home. Therefore, when they join the new family, they expect to continue with the same lifestyle, which may conflict with the new family.

Younger children are often seen as busy and playful. That may have been acceptable in their previous family, but it may not be acceptable for a new family that requires more quiet time because most members of the other family may be engaged in studies.

Cooking for children of different ages can be very challenging, even in a nuclear family. With a reorganized family, where the age range may be widely spread, cooking one meal that satisfies everyone may not be possible, but parents may not always have the money to prepare several different meals to meet the expectations of all of the children.

There are many positives about reorganized families, but the conflicts can be overwhelming. Parents have to be willing and able to find solutions for the reorganized family.

7. Problems with homeownership and landlords

Those who have constructed their property must be congratulated. It is never an easy investment to construct a personal dwelling place. However, not everyone is fortunate enough to construct their own dwelling property. There will always be rental properties, even if there is much land available.

Figure 7. Basic problems encountered in constructing a domestic dwelling property

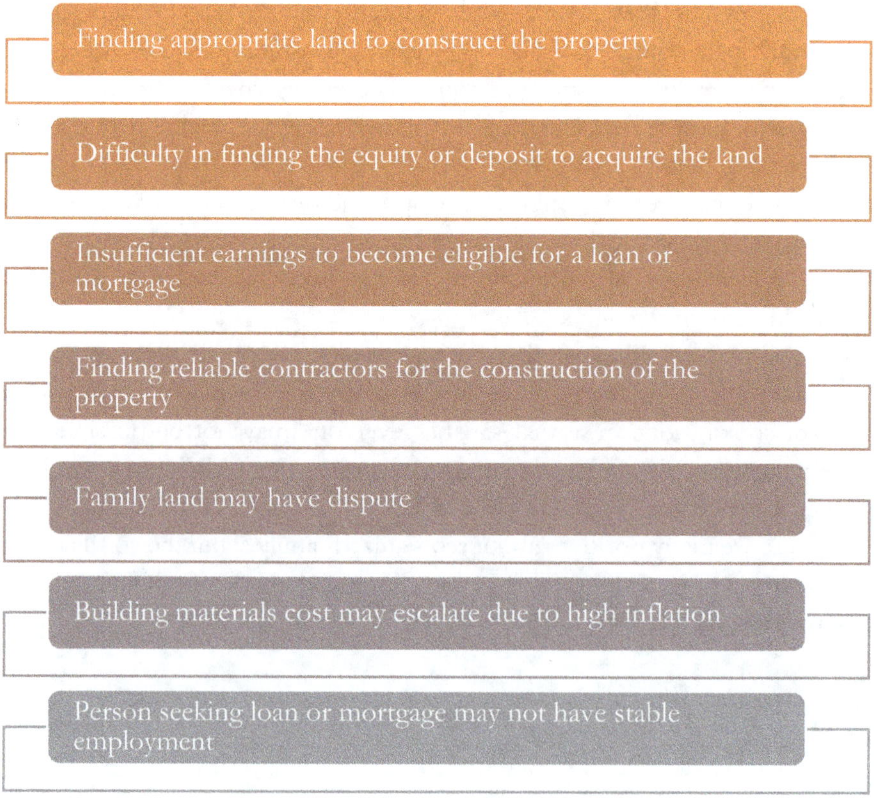

Finding appropriate land to construct the property

Difficulty in finding the equity or deposit to acquire the land

Insufficient earnings to become eligible for a loan or mortgage

Finding reliable contractors for the construction of the property

Family land may have dispute

Building materials cost may escalate due to high inflation

Person seeking loan or mortgage may not have stable employment

With the problems mentioned, it is evident why some persons will choose to rent a place. Renting must not be a permanent position, but it may fit the temporary needs of persons.

Sadly, some persons will live the rest of their lives in a rented place. They become comfortable with the rented property and do not wish to construct their own property.

7.1 Disputes among partners can prevent homeownership

There are times when both partners in a relationship will encounter difficulty in deciding whether to own or rent a property. One partner may think that it is too expensive to construct a property, while the other may think that the timing is not right to start the construction.

Sometimes, the compensation that one person is earning is not adequate to engage in a loan or mortgage. Therefore, both persons will have to agree to provide financial information to the bank to obtain a loan or mortgage. While one partner may agree to do this, the other partner may disagree.

There are persons who feel comfortable with living in a rented property. They see their parents living in a rented property and they feel that they must do the same thing themselves.

Land ownership in some countries may be difficult or impossible. Not all governments will make land easily accessible to citizens and non-citizens. In some communities, lands are mainly allocated for agricultural purposes, so they cannot be used for domestic dwellings, and therefore, loans will not be provided for those lands.

7.2 Tenant and landlord disputes

Some landlords do not care about people, but may only care about the amount of the money to be received. On the other hand, some tenants do not take care of properties and make it difficult for other potential tenants.

Table 2. Problems with tenants and landlords

Tenant problems	Landlord problems
Do not pay rent on time	Fail to maintain the property

Fail to maintain the property as stated in the rental agreement	Fail to insure the property
Additional persons may join the family without the knowledge of the landlord	Want to be involved in a tenant's personal life
Children may damage the property and infrastructure	Constantly increase the rent
Practice poor hygiene at the property	Are disrespectful to the tenant

There will continue to be disputes between tenants and landlords. Some of these disputes may not be for any significant issue, but both persons may have some differences which they fail to address.

When there are constant issues between the landlord and tenant, it can cause the tenants to become frustrated. The tenant may seek other options to change their dwelling, but may not be fortunate enough to do so. Not all tenants may have the money required to rent places where they are comfortable dwelling. To rent someplace, the tenant may have to provide a security deposit, which may be at least two months' rent. Not all tenants may have those funds, and they may find it frustrating to change dwellings even though they are uncomfortable with their current dwelling.

8. Problems with your vehicles

Vehicles are easy to acquire for some persons, yet many still do not own a vehicle. It takes some savings to acquire a vehicle or to borrow from the financial institution in order to acquire one. Decades ago, mainly the wealthy persons were able to own a vehicle. While some of them had at least two vehicles, the ordinary person continues to walk or take public transportation.

Figure 8. Ordinary person's progression to vehicle ownership

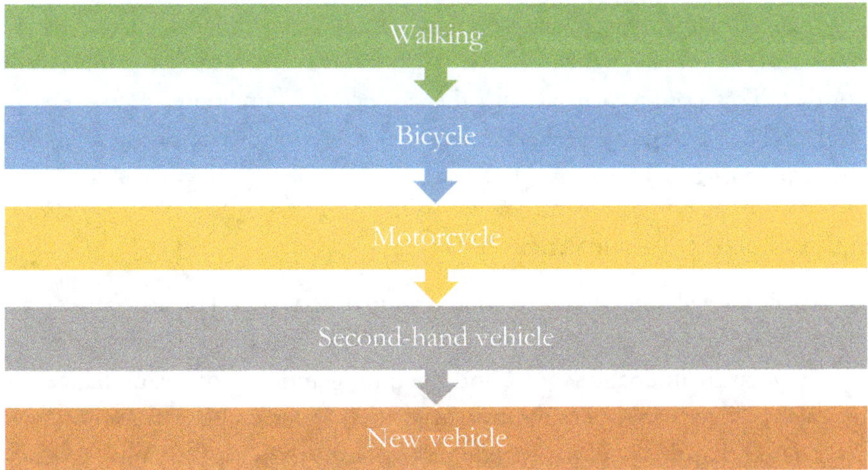

Some ordinary people may go through all of the processes mentioned in the diagram above, while others may skip some of them. Many children do not know that their parents had to endure these processes to make life better for them. Most children want a new vehicle at a very early age. They often expect that their parents will purchase the vehicle for them without any contribution from the children themselves. When parents have discussions with their children, they may remind them of these processes and tell the children how life has changed for them.

8.1 Loan repayment

Acquiring a loan is not always easy. Many financial institutions inform the public that they can access loans, but these loans can be very challenging for some persons to obtain. Most times, the client will have to provide a deposit. This deposit may be a fixed percentage, so the amount to be deposited will be based upon the value of the vehicle.

Borrowing to purchase a vehicle may be an easy process; however, the problem can be with the repayment. Many persons enjoy borrowing and making the first few installments, but continuing those payments for many years can become very challenging.

If a person took a loan to purchase a vehicle when they were young, and then start a family before they finish repaying the loan, then they will probably have less disposable income. With limited income, some expenditures will have to be prioritized. On some occasions, repayment of the installments may be challenging and persons will miss payments, which will cause the financial institution to take certain actions.

Constant inability to pay installments can cause the financial institution to repossess the vehicle, which will result in embarrassment and probably family conflict. This conflict can affect other aspects of family life. Also, persons who are unable to pay their installment may not concentrate properly in their work or studies.

8.2 Vehicle maintenance

An older vehicle often needs much maintenance. Those who cannot afford to purchase new vehicles will have to settle for older vehicles and may have regular maintenance to do, and the timing and cost of maintenance can be high. When some persons purchase their vehicles, they may not have considered that they will have frequent expenses to maintain their vehicles.

The poorly maintained vehicle can be embarrassing to persons. Just imagine a family going to a wedding, where everyone is well dressed, and the vehicle encounters mechanical issues and is unable to move. This situation, if not handled properly by the occupants of the vehicle, can become a serious embarrassment. Some persons in a relationship have many disagreements because the vehicle malfunctions while they are on their way to a destination. One argument leads to another, which may plague the family for a very long time.

Regular vehicle maintenance for old vehicles will reduce the family's disposable income. As the family increases, every dollar is important, so low maintenance cost is very important.

8.3 Vehicle insurance

Vehicle insurance is another expenditure that the vehicle owner has to pay. When persons were walking, they had no concern about vehicle insurance, but once they purchase an old or new vehicle, then they have to pay insurance.

Most times, the insurance premiums will be calculated based on the value of the vehicle. Therefore, the insurance cost for an older model vehicle will not be the same as a newer model.

Figure 9. Vehicle insurance payment periods

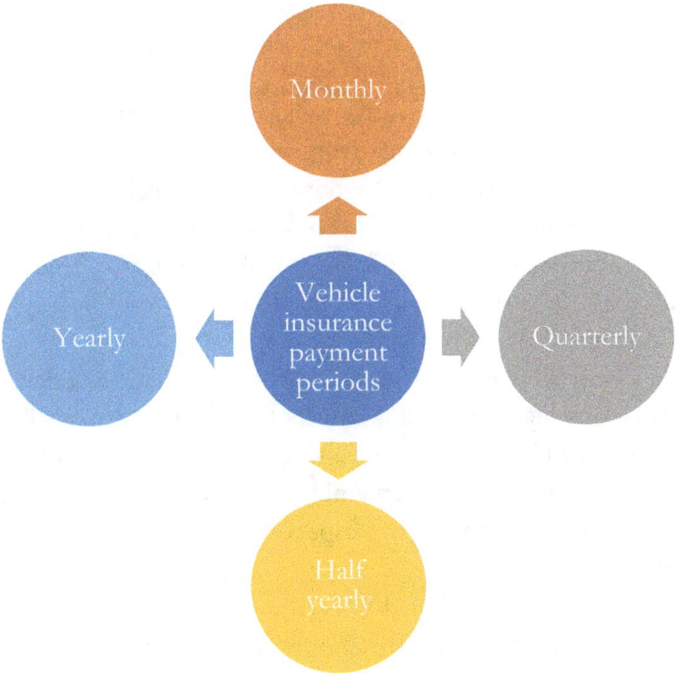

8.4 Vehicle accidents

No one wants their vehicle to be involved in an accident. Everyone hopes daily that they will reach their destination safely and return safely.

There are many drivers on the roadway; some are new drivers, while others have been driving for many years. All drivers are expected to use the road wisely and safely. However, not every driver will do so.

There are many reasons why accidents occur. Even very careful drivers will be involved in accidents, and they are often surprised.

When accidents occur, many lives are affected, and the impact of some accidents will change the lives of persons and families forever. For example, when an accident results in serious injuries or death of the main financier of the family, it causes the rest of the family to seek alternative means for survival. This can cause well-established families to be fragmented. If there are children in the relationship, those children may not be able to enjoy the love and financial support of the parent who was once there for them.

Some accidents cause families who were once rich to become poor, especially if the main financier dies or there are many legal battles to settle any liabilities resulting from the accident.

8.5 Traffic offences

Similar to vehicle accidents, drivers may commit a traffic offence while driving. These offences can range from minor to major. One such traffic offence is jumping the red light. Oftentimes, the traffic light will change, but there are a few seconds between one colour and the next. Some drivers will drive slowly while passing the traffic light, while others will speed across. The actions by these drivers can cause other drivers to react in ways that may breach traffic (road safety) regulations.

Traffic offences often have fines attached to them. Regular breach of traffic regulations may cause some drivers to lose their driver's license. The fines for a traffic offence can be expensive, and finding the money may be a challenge for some persons. Remember that every dollar that leaves the family treasury will hurt the family, especially if such money is not used for positive things.

All drivers are often reminded to use the road carefully. They must look out for those who may not be looking out for themselves or who do not care about how they use the roadway. Every effort must be exercised to avoid accidents, as every accident has some cost attached to it.

9. Loans and mortgages

No one owns the world of money, so they cannot do whatever they want, whenever they want, without considering the cost. Therefore, borrowing may be essential for some persons.

Some persons do not like to borrow, while others enjoy borrowing without considering that they have to repay the money promptly and probably with interest.

9.1 Collateral needed by financial institutions

Before a person approaches a financial institution to borrow, they are expected to have some form of collateral. Some financial institutions are flexible, depending on the amount that the borrower needs, or if the borrower has some funds with that financial institution. However, the financial institution must be reasonably assured that the borrower has provided enough evidence that they will be able to repay the sum borrowed.

The borrower must be willing to provide collateral to the financial institution if they want to access the loan or mortgage. In the case of a mortgage, the borrower must be willing to surrender their transport or lease.

Figure 10. Collateral required by lending institutions

9.2 Principal

With any amount borrowed, to use a simple explanation, the actual amount provided by the financial institution will be the principal. This will be the amount that the person or company needs. However, there are some cases where the borrower must possess part of the estimate needed, and the financial institution will provide the remaining amount. For example, if the borrower needs one hundred thousand dollars ($100,000), the financial institution may provide 75% of the amount requested. Therefore, the borrower is expected to find 25% of the $100,000, which will be twenty-five thousand dollars ($25,000).

One challenge for many persons is that they are unable to find the down payment or their equity. If they do not have enough funds to meet the equity, they may have to borrow from others or continue to save their money until they reach the required equity.

9.3 Interest

Interest rates for each financial institution vary. However, the borrower must always be willing to repay the principal plus the interest.

Many persons borrow a small amount and may want to take a long period to repay it. If the financial institution uses compound interest, then the longer the repayment period, the greater the amount that must be repaid.

Borrowers must be aware of the interest rate when choosing to borrow. They must not be willing to just accept the fact that they will be able to borrow the money; instead, they must seek a manageable interest rate.

9.4 Repayment period

Those who borrow are subject to a repayment period. Both parties must agree to the repayment period.

Figure 11. Who determines the repayment period?

Oftentimes, it is believed that only the financial institution determines the repayment period. On many occasions, however, the financial institution will provide some options to the client and the client can choose which repayment period is most appropriate. For example, in the case of mortgages, the financial institution may provide a repayment duration of ten (10) to thirty (30) years. The client is able to choose any repayment time frame within that range. Therefore, if the borrower earns a small compensation and has many other expenditures, then a long repayment period may be most appropriate.

When the borrower fails to repay the amount borrowed and also fails to repay promptly, then it will cause the financial institution to discuss certain actions. One such action may be to increase the repayment duration. However, another action may be to place the matter before the courts, and oftentimes, the last resort will be to repossess the asset or any valuables from the client. In cases of repossession, many borrowers and their families are placed in an embarrassing situation, which may cause some persons to take strange actions.

Section B: Overcoming your problems

While there are problems, there are also solutions. Persons sometimes think of committing suicide because they believe that they are the only ones who have problems. They become frustrated about their problems and want to give up.

However, there is hope. Do not give up! Your problems may look like a mountain, but with the right kind of support, you can overcome it. You cannot fight your problems all by yourself. Too many persons trust in their own strength and wisdom to overcome their problems. It must be noted that when persons have problems, they may not be able to find solutions easily.

Your family is a good source of assistance. Some family members may not be there for you, yet others may be willing to provide you with whatever assistance you need. Be courageous enough to let your family know of your problems, as they may be the best persons to assist you.

If you are working, your workmates will be another group of persons who will guide you to find solutions. Some of your workmates are very concerned about your success. If they have spent much time observing you, then as soon as they see some strange behaviours and actions from you, they will be willing to reach out to you. They do not need your money, but they want to assist you.

You will not always have the opportunity to tell persons about your problems, and when you do, those persons may not always have the appropriate answers for you. In such cases, listening to motivational songs is a good thing to do. As you listen to songs, you may find the inner strength to make wise decisions.

Increasing your learning is another good defence to your decision-making. Persons who are educated may give more thoughts about a positive decision. While some educated persons will still make poor decisions, they have access to quality information before making decisions.

Counsellors are there to assist persons. Your problems may not seem like anything strange to a counsellors. What you may see as a big problem may be a small problem to a counsellor, due to their experience of assisting other persons like you who were in similar situations.

To stay alive, against all of the negative things that are going through your mind, is to seek help. You may never know who will be there for you until you mention that you need help. It may be surprising to see the number of caring persons who will lend support to you, without expecting anything in return. Since other persons have overcome their problems, you will overcome your problems as well.

10. Talking with families

Never neglect to disclose your problems with your family members. They may be your first line of defence and may be able to offer workable solutions. They may not all agree with you on everything, but if they know that you have genuine problems, some of them will listen to you and share views that will help you.

10.1 Why talk with your family?

Some persons have certain trusted family members. As soon as something happens, they have family members to reach out to. Some family members do not need an invitation to know how you are progressing, since they are always checking to see how you are doing. They are not afraid to dial your telephone number and to call you regularly. They never consider the cost of the telephone call, but know that they must keep the family relationship together and that the relationship is more important than the cost.

Figure 12. Why share your problems with your family?

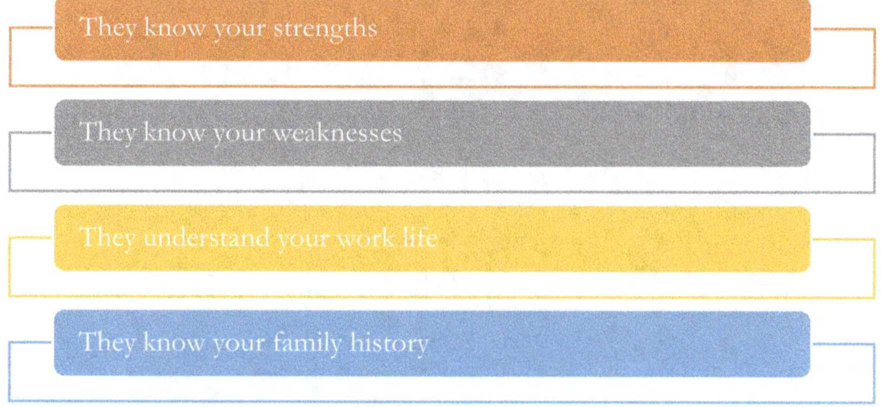

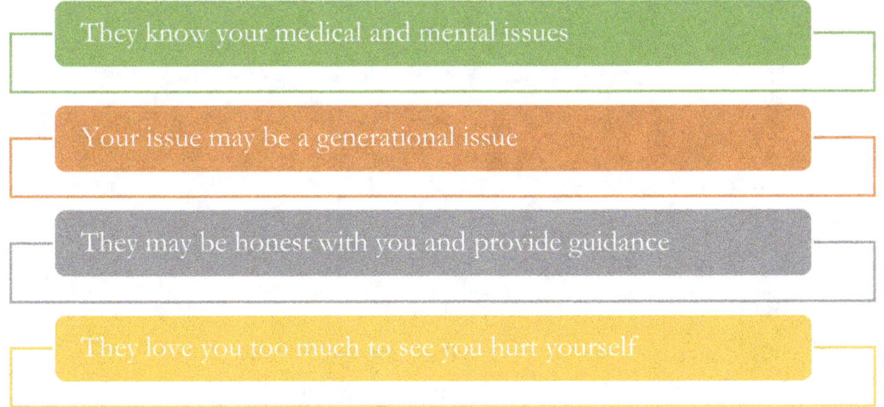

10.2 What to share with your family?

While many family members would like to know about your personal life, not all of them can keep things confidential, so some of them must only be provided with brief information, rather than detailed information.

Children sometimes may want to share information with their parents, but they may perceive their parents to be biased in their views. However, each child must keep their parents informed so that they can obtain parental advice.

Parents can also share some of their challenges with their children. It may not be appropriate to share certain information with young children who may not understand or be able to help. However, when children become adults, they may be able to provide that assistance to their parents.

Some families have members who are counsellors, teachers, and religious leaders. These individuals may have a wealth of experience and may be able to provide comfort and guidance to persons who are facing problems.

10.3 When to share with your family?

Do not wait until problems become so large that you cannot manage them before sharing them with family members. While you may not agree with the views they share with you, it is important to seek their assistance.

Let family members know that you need them, and they may be open to you. As you reach out to them, they may be able to provide much important information that will help you to overcome and become a champion. No single family member may have all the answers that you need. So, if you reach out to a few of them, their combined assistance may provide what you need.

11. Talking with friends

If you are going to win your battle against suicide, you have to be willing to talk. If you keep all of your problems to yourself, then you will constantly think that nobody cares about you.

11.1 Why talk with friends?

Not everyone has many friends. Surprisingly, some persons even have more enemies than friends. Sometimes, it is those enemies who will create more harm to a person who is suffering from depression. Enemies sometimes think of all of the negative things that are happening, and when they speak, the words released from their mouths can be toxic.

Everyone needs friends; even if you do not have many friends, any friends are good to have. Some friends can be as close as relatives.

Figure 13. Why share your problems with your friends?

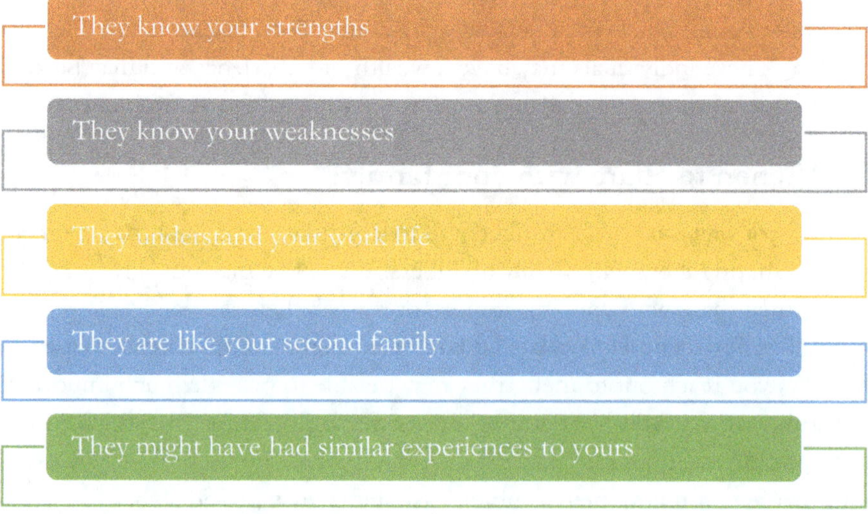

> They may be honest with you and provide guidance

> They love you too much to see you hurt yourself

In the diagram above, take note that many friends know your secrets and still care about you. They love you too much to see you take your life. They may be there to remind you of all the good times and assure you that you will overcome these problems.

There are some friends you are very familiar with since they might have lived in the same community or went to school together. You may also make friends in the workplace.

11.2 What to share with friends?

Not all friends are at the same level as you are in dealing with problems, so be careful about what you share with them. Some friends want to know much information, but there is no assurance that they will keep that information in confidence. During your time of distress, some persons will choose to become your friend because they want to learn about your problems in order to broadcast them to many other persons.

When a person establishes a friendship, they must not disclose all of their information to that person too soon. They first need to do some background checks on that new friend. It may be useful to progressively share certain information with someone and then wait for a while before deciding to share additional information. During the waiting period, listen to hear if any of the information shared was leaked.

Once the newfound friend has proven to be trustworthy, then that friendship will move to the next stage, where more information can be shared. That process will continue until you are satisfied that you do not have to second-guess yourself when sharing information with that friend.

When a friendship is mature, some detailed and personal information can be shared. You are free to share your personal feelings and frustration with such a friend. Even if some bedroom information is shared, it is assured that such information will not find its way into the public domain.

Therefore, when you are frustrated, reach out to those trusted friends and share with them about your frustration. Be open enough with them to let them know how you feel. They may provide a good shoulder for you to lean on.

If you are not honest, then no one will be able to help you. Tell them about your problem like it is, without feeling embarrassed. The more they know, the faster they may be able to help you and cause you to rethink your decision.

11.3 When to share with friends?

Good friends are always important to keep. As soon as you sense that you have a problem that you cannot resolve, then share it with those good friends, who can assist you. Never try to keep your problems to yourself if you know that you cannot resolve them on your own. Too many persons keep their problems to themselves and suffer from mental issues. Some of them made wrong decisions as a result, and their action caught many persons by surprise.

Whenever you sense that your problem is becoming overwhelming, reach out to your friends. Never wait until they reach out to you. Remember, you are the one who needs help. Let your friends know that you need help. They must know that it is not a time for sympathy, but a time where great assistance is needed. Give them the opportunity and liberty to assist you, since you are unable to help yourself at this stage.

To keep the friendship, do not only share with them when you have problems, but also when you have success. Never be the person who, when your friends see you, they know that you have problems. You must be someone they always want to see, and they must always be happy to hear from you. They must never predict you. When the friendship is very good, do not keep them out of your life's progress. Once you sense that there is a problem and you are unsure of what to do, make contact with your friends, share your feelings, and get their professional advice. It is better to work with the advice of many, rather than regret the decision of a lone ranger. Tell your problems to your trustworthy friends early and save your life.

12. Listening to motivational music

Songs can be like medicine, as they can soothe and heal a person's emotions. Songs do not discriminate against persons who choose to listen to them. Anyone can choose a song and enjoy the emotional response that the songs provide to them.

12.1 Songs motivate without considering age restriction

Anyone who is having problems, whether young or old, can listen to songs. Some of the same songs are enjoyed by young persons and those who are in their senior years. At some entertainment places, there is a mixture of young and not so young persons, because they all enjoy the same songs. While some persons drive to work, they may spend most of their time listening to the songs they choose.

There is never an age restriction when it comes to problems: both young and old persons have them. Students who attend school have problems with learning and sometimes their teachers, as do adults who attend school. Both children and adults who want to learn can also listen to songs.

The beautiful thing about songs is that they can penetrate beyond the skin and affect your emotion. Many persons depend upon songs to put them in a mood to become better. Not everyone likes to be worried, and so they will choose songs that will motivate and soothe them.

12.2 Patients recover by listening to songs

While every patient will recover at different rates, some persons recover faster when they listen to songs. They continue to take their medication, but they also listen to songs while they lie in bed. The songs they listen to often speak to their emotions and remind them that each day is worth living for. Those songs may remind them of the days when they were in better health.

Families of some patients will rent a private room in the hospital so that their family can listen to songs without distracting other patients. As they listen to the songs, their minds are moved from their problems and now focus on their recovery.

Members of some religions believe that when they listen to certain songs, it helps with healing. Therefore, arrangements will be made for the patient to hear these religious songs while they are sick.

12.3 The song drives away the fear

Many songs have the potential to drive away fear. For example, when a person thinks that they are a failure and will not be successful, if they listen to the right songs, they may soon recognize that they have what it takes to win and succeed.

Songs can reinforce the confidence in some persons that today they will be victorious. Fear is often present when victory is ahead of a person. For example, even the best performing student in a class may still be fearful when approaching the examination, even though they have prepared for it. However, after the examination, the student will soon recognize that their fear has gone.

With the right choice of songs, a person's fear quickly subsides. They soon recognize that they are the victor and not the victim.

Before some persons start their day of work, they may play songs. Those who have a strong religious background will choose songs that will uplift their spirit. These songs may be played after they have their morning devotion. Those who own their vehicles may continue to play those religious songs on their way to work.

It is always important to have a positive attitude when you have to work, and songs can help with this. As some persons work, they may sing the songs they like. However, they must ensure that their singing does not distract others. One person's celebration may be another person's problem.

Those who listen to songs while they work must play their songs at a modest volume. At some workplaces, employees will not be allowed to listen to songs, and that is understood. But for those who work in an office all by themselves, there may be no restriction for them as it relates to what they listen to and when. Even so, employees must remain ethical in what they do. They must be diligent with their work and not allow the songs to negatively affect their performance. Persons can become so engrossed in songs that their performance decreases. That is not what any organization expects of its employees.

12.4 Different songs, different response

Certain songs will have different responses from different persons. It is interesting to see that when some persons listen to particular songs, they appear to have a revival. They begin to have a smile on their face. Instead of being an introvert, they suddenly begin to operate as an extrovert.

Persons who attend gyms will recognize that many of the gym instructors or trainers will have songs playing in the background. As the songs are played, the trainee will continue to exercise, sometimes not even realizing how much they are training or how much time has passed.

In some supermarkets and food marts, selected songs are played. As the customers continue their shopping, they will listen to the songs and may shop for more than they had planned to purchase, as the songs give them a joyful feeling.

For persons who are depressed and often have problems, if they listen to the right songs, they soon become emotionally stronger. It may take just one song to make someone know that they can and will overcome every thought of suicide.

12.5 Listen and dance

As you listen to songs, you may feel the urge to dance. You are not required to be a professional dancer to dance; anyone can dance in order to have some fun and ease their emotional tension. When many persons finish dancing, they have a different mindset, and those problems which once stood in front of them as mountains have now become a valley. As they burn energy, they may also be inclined to look at their problems from a different angle.

If persons want to dance, they must be prepared to exert energy, as some songs demand many movements. The person who wants to sing and dance along with the song must wear appropriate clothing and footwear. With all of the movements when dancing, there is less need for anything that may be a distraction.

In some communities, some persons are often counting down until the weekend. The reason why they do this is that they want to go to a place of entertainment where they can listen to songs and dance. Some job relationships are stressful. With these highly stressful lives, those who cannot manage the stress will seek every opportunity to have some fun as they listen to songs and dance.

During weekends, some persons who have to wash their clothing may have songs playing in the background. As the songs are played, they may dance and sing along while they wash the clothes. They may choose songs that allow them to ease their tension and give them the motivation to finish their laundering.

12.6 Songs enhance romantic relationships

Every relationship between two companions will have problems. Some of those problems are very easy to resolve, but others require more attention and can only be resolved over a longer period of time.

When someone in a relationship knows that they have problems, they may choose some songs to listen to. Based on their state of depression, they may play the songs quietly or loudly. If they feel very connected, they may attempt to sing the songs, even if they are unfamiliar with all of the lyrics.

When persons are enjoying their courtships, they may go to entertainment places where they can build their relationship. Many of those places may have an option for songs to be played. As the songs play in the background, both persons will continue to communicate. Even when persons are in their vehicles or building their sensual relationship, they will have songs of their choice played.

If there is disagreement within the home, one of the companions may choose to play a particular song. As the song plays, both persons may forget their problems and begin to build their relationship once again. Probably, within a short time, both persons will be back together as though they never had problems.

12.7 Songs enhance learning

Educators and parents may play songs that students like, which helps to enhance their learning. For toddlers and teenagers alike, some of their learning materials may include songs that they like. For example, if they have to learn through the use of videos, then the videos may include some songs before, during, or after the content of the video.

As students listen to those songs, they are motivated to learn and pay much attention to the materials provided to them. When some persons are studying for examinations, they may have songs playing in the background as they study. Some persons even say that they are unable to study effectively without songs.

13. Increase your learning

While many persons may feel depressed and want to give up, they must not give up on their learning. Some persons' problems can be combated by increasing their learning. When people's learning increases, they see many opportunities.

Frustrated persons often believe that they are the only person who may be going through their problems, but as they learn more, they will recognize that many other persons are experiencing the same things. Once they know that they are not alone, then they can share their ideas with others and also seek help.

Uneducated persons can be harmful to themselves, while those who have learned may look for solutions rather than problems.

13.1 Learning through reading

Those who want to motivate themselves must be willing to gather important information. One important way to do that is to spend time reading. Not everyone will be disciplined enough to learn through reading, but reading provides great help to persons who need to know more.

Government ministries, like the Ministry of Health, Education, Labour, and Social Protection, will usually provide written information that will help persons who are frustrated and thinking of harming themselves. The information is geared towards letting persons know that there are alternative ways of addressing their concerns. Some workplaces will receive the information from one of these agencies, which will be circulated, giving persons guidance on how to win the battle against suicide.

13.2 Learning through watching

As mentioned above, not everyone likes to read. If some persons are given the opportunity, they would prefer to sit and watch most of the things that they have to learn. When a person chooses to learn by watching videos or television programs, they also provide themselves with the opportunity to learn.

The websites of some organizations provide videos with essential information for clients and persons who are affected by problems. Since the videos are online, anyone who can access the website will be able to watch them. Not every office may be able to have employees working twenty-four hours per day, so they may have some of their information available through videos.

Interestingly enough, some organizations may have a television series that provides persons with advanced information. In cases where a community is known for regular suicide, those television series will target those communities with messages that will help them to have a positive view of life. The television series may provide many alternatives for persons to consider.

Those organizations that are making great attempts to help persons stay alive must be commended. While persons may be overwhelmed by their problems, someone must be there for them ahead of time.

Every life that is lost, whether by suicide or accident, is important. While an accident often happens swiftly, persons often give some time and attention when contemplating suicide. Therefore, if someone or something can capture their attention early, then it can prevent them from making that regrettable mistake.

13.3 Learning through listening

Learning opportunities never cease, and listening is another way to help persons to learn. Within some rural areas, there may be limited access to reading materials or televisions. Therefore, they may be restricted to listening to radios. Through the radio programs, quality information will be provided to them, which will give them hope.

Once again, some of the ministries and Non-Governmental Organizations (NGO) will provide audio information to the public. This will be preventative information to help persons who are considering suicide. Special actors or influential persons may be recruited to share positive news, which gives hope to persons who are frustrated and depressed. The use of influential persons may encourage more persons to pay attention or to listen to the audio sessions. With that encouragement, depressed persons may find hope in themselves.

14. Seek counselling

Persons who are having problems often feel that they can solve their problems by themselves. They do not want anyone to know that they are having problems, so they keep everything to themselves, which can be dangerous.

14.1 Why seek counselling?

The main reason why you must seek counselling is that you may be unable to help yourself during this current state. When a medical doctor becomes sick and needs surgery, he or she will seek help from other professional doctors who can perform the surgery.

Too many persons feel that they can diagnose and fix their problems. Help is available, but some persons think that their problems will soon end on their own.

Figure 14. Why seek counselling?

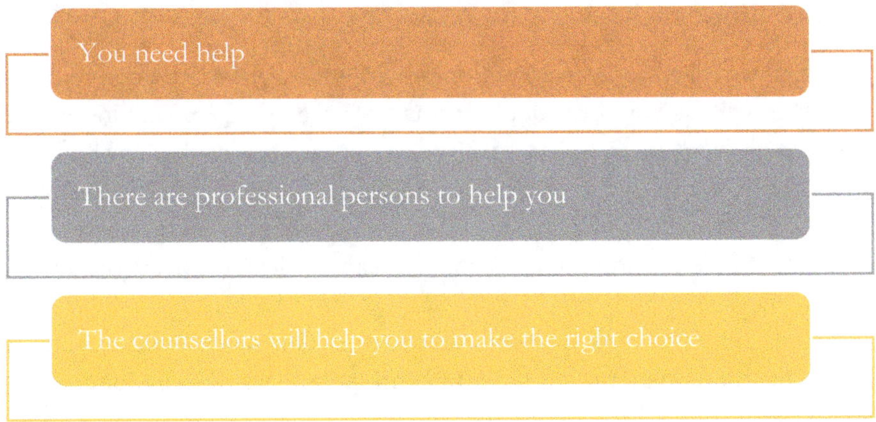

> Many persons love you and want to be your friend

> At your current stage, you are thinking of negative things

14.2 Professional counselling is needed

When some persons are having problems, they feel that it is their responsibility to tell only their friends and family. It is good that they share their problems with others. However, they must also talk with those who will be able to offer professional assistance.

Family and friends have their limitations, but professional counsellors are trained to assist in a specific area. What may take family and friends a long time to resolve, many professional counsellors can resolve quickly.

For example, a civil engineer and an electrical engineer have two different skill sets. They both might have done some of the same basic courses, but in their final years of learning, they specialize in different areas. That final year makes a great impact on their careers and gives them advantages over other persons who are not specialists in those fields. Therefore, when choosing a counsellor, choose one who specializes in areas that will enable them to offer the appropriate assistance.

14.3 Be honest

When you need assistance, be honest with those who are trained to assist you. They will ask you some questions. Do not provide them with inaccurate answers. *Tell them the truth.* Even if they do not ask a particular question, but you know that the information is important for them to know, be open enough to share the truth with them. Remember, they are there to assist you.

Lack of proper and timely information can result in incorrect diagnoses, which may be harmful to you. Many persons who are having domestic problems often try to cover up those problems. This will only hurt them for longer periods and may cause them to harm themselves, since no one knows and no one will be able to assist them.

14.4 Follow their process and guidance

Remember that the professional counsellor is trained. They may have to follow a code of ethics and a code of conduct. Therefore, the information they share with you, once it is used according to the process they have mentioned, will work for you.

For example, some persons visit a medical doctor due to ill health, and the doctor provides them with some medication. For the first few days, they begin to use the medication, but they stop taking it before their health improves. After a short period, they become sick again with the same issue. On this second occasion, the medication previously issued and the dosage may not be appropriate. They may have to also incur more costs for something that they could have prevented from the beginning.

Figure 15. Follow professional guidance and provide feedback

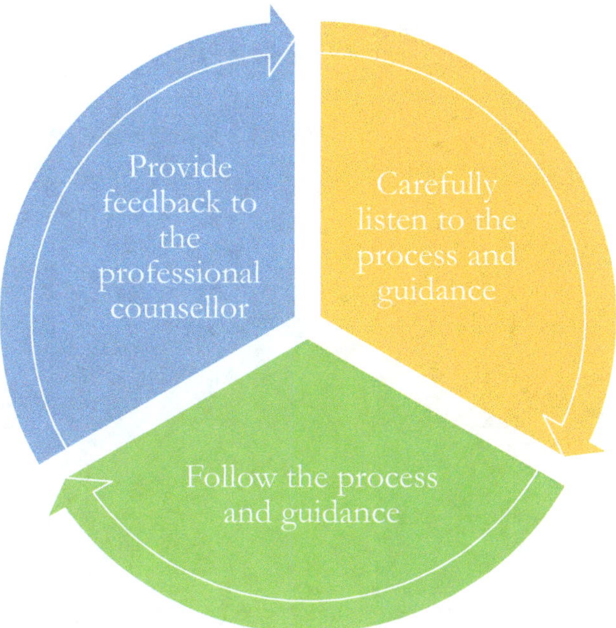

Many persons wait until they are very sick before they can visit a doctor, but it is good to visit the doctor just to have a basic checkup. Similarly, it is always important to follow the professional counsellor's guidance. After you have done all that they advised you to do, provide the counsellor with updates. Do not wait to communicate with the professional counsellor until you become a patient once again with the same issue that once affected you.

Section C: Rejoicing

You had problems, you sought help, and now you are a winner. Your problems were many, but you also had much support. You now know that you are victorious, and if a similar situation occurs again, you are willing to take on such a challenge and come out victorious.

Knowing that you have made it is always a great feeling. Do you know that many persons were not as successful as you? Some persons give in to the feeling and give up on life, even making shocking decisions.

Not everyone is willing to wait for the storms to pass them by. As soon as a storm seems to be approaching, some persons believe that it will be the end of their days. There will always be storms, but those who overcome are champions.

Now that you have overcome your problems, begin to celebrate. Your celebration can be small or big, but be willing to celebrate.

There are great opportunities ahead of you after overcoming your problems. Those who quit on life do not have the opportunity to see what you can see. They are unable to meet family members and celebrate their anniversaries.

When a person takes their own life, they are no longer able to work. If your work is stressful, then change the work or the organization. Once those problems are behind you, then celebrate, as a new employer may be your best choice for a great future. Some employers may have thought that you were not good for them, but other employers will be so happy for you to work for them, and they will be willing to offer you better compensation. Do not allow your employer to make you feel that you are a loser. While you may have to adjust some of the things that you are doing so that your performance will improve, work towards improving yourself.

Are you in good health? If your answer is yes, then rejoice. Many persons would like to trade their health for yours. While they may have much money, their money cannot restore their health.

Take some time to thank your supporters. Without your supporters, you might have been dead if you had followed your negative thoughts. Your supporters may be many, but show them all your appreciation, since they thought it was important for you to stay alive.

You are a champion. You have overcome. Therefore, go and help others. Many persons are struggling like you once did. They may not know how to overcome their problems and are looking for someone like you who understands their situation. Those who have had a similar experience may be more impactful than those who are providing theoretical answers.

15. You have made it

When someone has overcome depression and chosen not to accept suicide as their option, they have won their mental battle. Too often, frustrated persons will think that they have to take their own lives, and even that they are doing something good by making that choice. Sadly, they do not know that they are harming themselves and many other persons who depend upon them.

Life will never be without problems, regardless of a person's faith and status. It may seem that problems look for people, but people must be wise enough to win their battle against their problems. There are often many solutions, but not everyone will choose the best one.

Today, you have made your choice. You are alive. You must be congratulated. It was not an easy decision, but you chose wisely. Do you know how many persons are waiting to celebrate with you?

15.1 Avoid similar problems

There will be many similar situations in the future, but now that you have made it, you can make it on future occasions. There will always be problems, but what will be your response?

It is important to be mindful of problems that are similar to what you have already faced and overcome. Some of them are obvious and do not require much thinking to know them. Those problems may have traits similar to what you have overcome in the past. There will also be some strange problems that you have never experienced before.

Whether your problems are new or old, your motive must be to win. If you win today, you can also win tomorrow.

15.2 Think of positive solutions for future problems

Do not live your life thinking about problems. Keep your mind thinking of positive solutions. Sometimes there may be only a few solutions that you can think of, but keep thinking positively.

It takes too much energy to spend quality time thinking negatively. There is no benefit in thinking negatively, since some of those fears will never occur. People sometimes spend too much time thinking of things that will not occur to them. One such example is fear of death. While everyone will eventually die, do not exert energy thinking of death. What might be more important is to put systems in place so that in the event you die suddenly, persons will not be worse off because of your sudden death.

16. Great opportunities ahead of you

You cannot change yesterday. Therefore, be your best for today.

Persons often have regrets about what happened in the past, or even hate to remember it. Whenever they give thought to the past, tears come to their eyes and they are sad. For example, persons who have gone through domestic problems often hate to remember those problems, since those problems stand like obstacles to their future. Sometimes, it is evident that persons who have had an unfortunate situation will quickly become depressed when similar situations occur. Those who survived a horrific accident, for example, will often become emotional when they see a similar situation. It sometimes brings everything to their memory as though the event happened yesterday.

Yesterday is gone. You cannot change anything about yesterday. While the memories may be bad, you must live beyond yesterday.

16.1 A new day, a new opportunity

Each day has its problems and opportunities. Yesterday might have been the day with many bad experiences, but today can be the day with great opportunities.

Figure 16. Looking back at your problems will be harmful to your future success

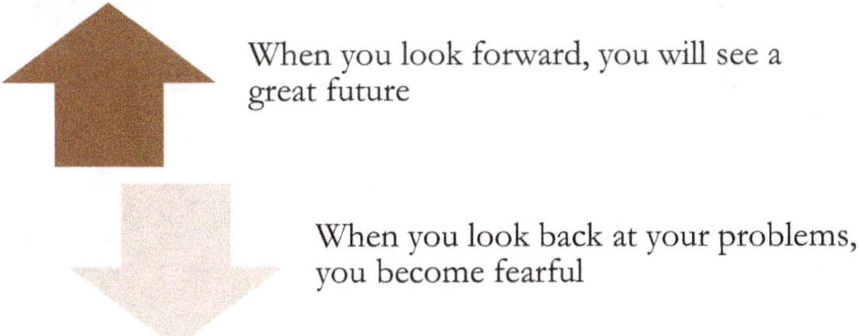

Live for today and not yesterday, as you cannot change yesterday, but you can change today. Take all of the energy that you have and make today one of the best days that you have ever embraced. You may not always feel great on a particular day, but each day has great potential. All of what you are expecting may not unfold immediately, but it can be sooner than you anticipate.

Keep thinking and acting positively. Give your energy today towards good things. Let yesterday's problems rest in yesterday and take on a new posture for today.

Each day, wear your best clothes, as if you have an appointment with a great person. When you speak with people, speak as though you are the champion.

One way of overcoming fear is through constant positive thinking. For instance, if you have to attend an interview, except that the outcome will be positive.

Never lose sight of the fact that life has many good things to offer to you. While bad things will happen, you must not spend your energy and time thinking that bad things will happen to you.

17. You are employed

If you are employed, then rejoice. Do you know how many other persons are desperately seeking employment? You may not have everything that you would like to have, but you can rejoice that someone saw you as a good enough person to provide you with an employment opportunity.

17.1 Earning for yourself

There is often a joy in earning for yourself. When this happens, you are less dependent upon others, and in some cases, you even have the opportunity to financially support those who once supported you. So, the desire to overcome suicide and stay alive allows you to receive a reward for your labour.

Those who took their lives cannot contribute to society. They are unable to work and earn for themselves. Within some families, the person who was depressed and wanted to take their life was the main financier for the family. Had that individual chosen to do something wrong, then the rest of the family could have been fragmented.

Many children lose their focus and dream when one of their parents commits suicide. Not only do the children lose their parents, but they also lose someone who contributed financially to the family.

It is not only poor and unemployed persons who commit suicide. There are also many wealthy and employed persons who make that tragic mistake. After their life is gone, many persons are made to suffer. If they had just thought about the negative impact of their decision, then they would have made a positive decision to stay alive.

17.2 Ability to meet positive-thinking workmates

Working can be very challenging, yet it can also be very joyful. Some persons go to work not because of the money, but because they find their work environment to be a place that provides them with therapy for their stress. They have the opportunity to laugh and talk with people.

The employees at their workplace are like their family. Everyone looks out for each other. Someone remembers their birthday or anniversary. Those who are successful in an examination may receive many congratulations and sometimes monetary rewards.

Not all supervisors will treat employees like kings and queens. However, there are some supervisors who love people and will often communicate positively with them. Some supervisors will protect their employees and listen to their concerns if the employee chooses to voluntarily share their concerns.

When some supervisors know that an employee is having family problems or another issue that will affect their productivity, the supervisor will adjust that employee's work so that the employee will still be able to be effective. There are some caring and concerned supervisors who have great hope for their subordinates. Some supervisors will suggest that the troubled employee proceed on vacation, or they may suggest counsellors who will be able to assist the troubled employee. Thanks should be extended to these caring supervising officers.

17.3 Less time to think about problems

As you work, you have more time to think about good things and less time to think about bad things. Too many times, when persons are not meaningfully occupied, they have much time to think of negative things. However, those who are working know that their work may keep them occupied and may provide them with much laughter.

Within an organization, there may be someone who is a motivator. While others are having unpleasant days, that person can put smiles on their faces. Some of these motivators do not even realize how much stress they have removed from the employees who were depressed.

Life has many problems, and those who marry themselves to problems will recognize that they will only hurt themselves. However, when they come into contact with a workmate who will motivate them, they will soon forget about their problems and look for opportunities.

17.4 Concerned and motivating customers

Not all customers will cause unease to employees, but there may be some known customers that employees do not want to attend to, since they always appear to be impatient and unwilling to understand that all the employees want to do their professional duties. Even when employees are doing their work in a professional and timely manner, the customers often seem unsatisfied.

However, not all customers are like this. Some customers count it a joy to find out how the employees are doing. If it is not against the organization's policies for employees to receive gifts from customers, some customers will present gifts to employees. For example, with small organizations or small departments, some customers will celebrate their birthday with the employees by sharing some gifts and goodies with them. This action by the customer is never to obtain favour for future activities; these customers are ethical and will not do anything that will give them an unfair advantage for the future. If a customer's child is getting married, they may even invite certain employees to the wedding, due to the relationship that has developed between the customer and the employees.

Some of these motivational customers will share light and joyful moments with the employees when they visit the store. Some former customers may no longer be mobile but will still call, just to check and see how the employees are doing and to say some good words to them.

Working has its advantages and disadvantages, but those who find joy in working often enjoy being at work. These employees know that their place of employment is a safe place where they do not have to think about problems, but about great opportunities.

17.5 Acknowledging employees' performance

At some organizations, there may be a norm that an employee's success is celebrated by their co-workers. For example, a mother who has given birth can expect a gift, a card, and a reward. Some of the employees may also go beyond what the organization has done and make their own contributions.

Another example is that employees who have contributed to the success of the organization may be recognized as "Employee of the Month" or "Employee of the Year." This recognition is to honour those whose performances were notably outstanding. Many employees look forward to receiving this recognition. At some organizations, the photograph of such an employee will be placed somewhere in the building, so that other employees and customers can also acknowledge the employee whose performance was outstanding.

18. Good health

Everyone wants to have good health. However, having much money is not a guarantee that a person's health will be restored. Even having the best medical doctor does not always mean that your health will be restored, especially if you have health problems.

So, if you are in good health, then rejoice. Feel good about your health and celebrate. Many persons would like to improve their health, but they have not found success, despite their best effort. Many persons may want to give up on life, but if they are to reconsider, they will realize that many other persons are not in good health as they are.

18.1 Fewer expenses to pay

Those whose health is not where they want it to be often have many expenses to incur. Some of those persons will frequently visit the doctor, with the intention that their health will improve soon. They sometimes continue to spend lots of money, but with little improvement. Many elderly persons have to visit doctors frequently, and for each visit, they will have to incur some expenses. Some of those elderly persons may not have all the money needed, but their children will assist them financially.

However, those whose health is good must celebrate. It is surprising that some persons whose health is good will choose to take their own lives. While they may have many problems that they are unable to resolve by themselves, they must be thankful for their good health. We must remember that there is always something to be thankful for.

What many persons need to do is to visit the hospital and have a look at some of the patients there. Many of them are having major health issues, yet they still have hope that life will become better soon. Some of them wish that they could trade their body with those who have good health but do not recognize how fortunate they are.

18.2 Your good health may motivate someone

You may never know it, but your good health may be a motivator for someone. Many persons may long to be comfortable with their health. Being reminded of this fact should cause you to celebrate your good health. While your health may not be perfect, it is not the worst.

Take some time to exercise, in order to keep yourself in good shape. If you are unable to exercise on a routine basis, then seek alternative times to continue exercising. As you age, exercise will remain important.

Eating healthy meals is also important. Too many persons become joyful with their good health and choose not to follow their nutritional guidelines. However, you do not have to follow other persons who ignore their diet. Eat healthy and your days on earth may be very long.

Eating healthy may be costly, but it is the better thing to do. Eating healthy will keep you away from the doctor longer, as you continue to celebrate your health. Do not become overconfident, but monitor your health regularly.

19. Thank your supporters

Remember to thank your supporters. While you were going through your problems, there were many persons at your side. They have motivated you and encouraged you to stay alive. They were able to walk you from frustration to success.

19.1 Your family

During your time of problems, your family was at your side. They provided a shoulder for you to lean on. They listened to your concerns, heard your frustration, and told you that you do not have to hurt yourself. Even though you had disagreed with them, you now recognize that they love you and wanted to see the best out of you. They were willing to sacrifice long hours just to hear from you. When you cried, they cried too, as they wanted to see you overcome your problems.

Since they did so much for you when you were only thinking to hurt yourself, show them some gratitude. Visit them and express your appreciation for their support.

19.2 Your friends

Some friends are like family. They know most of your life stories. They are there with you when many others forsake you. Even when you disagree with them and refuse to communicate with them, they continue to pray for you and call you.

There are times when the friendship hits a tough spot, but they are still willing to reach out to you. They are willing to hold your hands and walk you through your problems. They remain confidential and do not share your private matters with anyone. These are persons that you must thank and show your appreciation for, especially during your challenging moments.

19.3 Your workmates

Not all workmates will be there for you. However, there are some who will not let you go. They will not allow you to fail. They knew that you had problems, as they saw strange behaviours from you. As they listened to you, they shared positive things about life and encouraged you to live again. They never accepted or supported your desire to commit suicide.

Many of these good workmates talked you out of your negative thinking. They listened to you and showed you the beauty and benefits of staying alive. Please show your appreciation to them.

19.4 Your neighbours

Neighbours sometimes know many things about you and take note of your actions and behaviours. They may also know the persons who visit you and how long they spend at your premises. Due to their observant nature, they may know when you are having problems. Sometimes, they may be the first ones to be at your side.

Not all neighbours are kind. However, those who assisted you must be remembered and thanked. Even if you do not do too many things for them, show them some appreciation for their commitment and support to you.

19.5 Your counsellor and religious leaders

Those who have overcome their problems might have interacted with a professional counsellor or a religious leader. These persons devoted some time to listen to the person who felt that they could not live anymore.

The conversation with a counsellor can go in different directions at different times. On some occasions, the counsellor may hear some strange stories and life experiences, which they cannot repeat due to their confidential nature. Some persons who want to give up their life can become confrontational, since they have already planned to end their life, thinking that all of their problems will be over. Therefore, since they have made up their minds, they do not want anyone to stop them from executing their well-orchestrated plans. They feel that nobody should have known that they were going to end their life.

Counselling people has never been easy work. Some religious leaders who also provide counselling sessions can be drained of energy when they hear the stories of persons who want to take their life.

However, there is always hope. No life was lost, and you are alive. Therefore, thank the counsellor or religious leader for persuading you to change your plan and stay alive.

20. You are another champion

Now that you have overcome, you are a champion. The problems were many, but you have prevailed. There were days when you felt like giving up, but you remained firm that you will stay alive.

The battle against suicide is over. The battle between negative and positive thoughts is over. Choosing life was a very important decision.

Some persons may not see you as a champion, but only you knew what you went through. Looking back at your journey, you had the option to fall prey to your failing. It might have been an easy decision for some persons to allow their suicidal thoughts to prevail. However, you made a good decision to win your battle against every suicidal thought.

Your inner strength prevailed. The assistance provided by your friends and family has allowed you to be victorious.

The looks on your face are brighter. More persons are now happy to associate with you. Members of your family are willing to celebrate your success, and others are talking about your success journey. You may never know the number of lives that you've touched when you choose to stay alive. Your testimony will be a great motivator for others who will be inclined to make a great decision just like you did.

Those persons who gave in and allowed their suicidal thoughts to defeat them are no longer able to celebrate. In the grave lie many persons who had great potential. Some of them would still be alive today if they had received the same support that you did. Many of them kept their problems to themselves and never let other persons know that they needed help.

In the grave are many who seemed like persons to admire, since they always looked good on the outside. Some of them had a beautiful attitude. So, they were beautiful on the outside, but inside, they were unable to resist the feeling to take their life.

As you reflect on your life, know that you made a good decision to stay alive. You are a champion. While you may not be given a trophy, you are a champion.

Few persons can have a feeling of wanting to take their life and resist that feeling. Some families and friends are still hurting because of the decisions that others took to end their lives. However, you and your family can celebrate your decision. You can now celebrate another birthday and another anniversary.

If you are earning for yourself, then take some time and celebrate like a champion. Some persons need others to tell them that they are champions, but with what you did in overcoming your problems, you can know for yourself that you are more than a champion.

21. Helping others to overcome

Now that you are a champion, help others who face the same challenges you have overcome. Give them the support they need to find strength and make the right decision to stay alive.

Many persons are suffering from suicidal thoughts, but they are unable to find anyone to help or advise them. Be willing to let persons know that you are there and they can seek your assistance. Let them know that you are not an expert, but you have made an important decision that suicidal thoughts were not going to win over you.

21.1 Share your story

Not everyone will know what you went through, so do not be afraid to share your story. At first, you may be timid and hesitant to let persons know that you were once contemplating suicide. Be honest with them and share that important information.

Allow persons to ask questions. While you may not have all the answers, tell them what you know. In cases where you do not know, be unafraid to admit that you do not know. If you can direct them to others who can help, then share such information with them, so that they will overcome.

21.2 Be an advocate

Become a person who looks for opportunities to provide others with information to make the right choice to win their battle against suicide. If it means that you have to establish a group, then do so. You may need the help of others to establish such a group, so seek their help.

Once the group is established, then promote it so that persons will become aware of it. There may be a need to seek some sponsorship to help promote your group. Your group may also need the support of government, Non-Government, or religious organizations. Be willing to seek wider support, as those other agencies may have a broader reach and may also have more finances.

If possible, have your group registered, so that it becomes an official group. With a registered group, there may be a possibility for financial support. There are other established groups, whether within the country or overseas, who may be willing to give their support. Some of those groups may also take time to promote your group.

With the wide use of social media, it may be easy for your group to be promoted and get further recognition. Members of the group must also be willing to be identified with and share information about the group.

Each member of the group must know that they have an active role to play in helping to promote it. In some cases, members may work towards branding the group, by wearing uniforms that represent the group. As they wear those uniforms, persons will be able to easily connect with them and seek their assistance.

Whenever there is an opportunity to do so, go to places and promote the group. Many persons need help against suicide, but they will not all come and state that they need help. Therefore, the more the group can reach out to them, the more it will help persons to be more open and to share their concerns.

There are some persons who are just waiting for someone to approach them concerning their problems. Let your group be one that reaches people who need to win their battle against suicide.

21.3 Promote others who overcame

When persons have overcome their battle with suicidal thoughts, then promote them. As you begin to help other persons to celebrate life and not death, then many persons who are depressed will choose life.

Many persons are looking for the testimonies of someone who has overcome suicide, and probably someone that they know. Successful persons can share their testimonies in written or verbal form. Some persons may not be able to or have the aptitude to read, so they will be happy to listen to those testimonies, while others will be happy to spend time reading information shared by someone who has overcome their battle against suicide.

There is a need for more persons to share their stories of victory against suicide. If many persons choose to share their stories, they may captivate many listeners, as there may not be any perfect way for each individual member to share their story.

More persons need to stay alive. Can you help someone to win their battle against suicide? If so, then provide your support and save an important life today. Give someone the hope and reassurance that although life has many problems, they can overcome, just like you have overcome. Say goodbye to death through suicide, and yes to life through positive thinking.

Reference List

Ramsawak, R., & Umraw, R.R. (2001). *Modules in Social Studies with SBA guide and CXC questions*. Caribbean Educational Publishers, 49 High Street, San Fernando, Trinidad, West Indies, ISBN 976-8014-06-7.

About the Author

Suicide is something that affects many persons. Many persons are crying out for help, hoping that someone will quickly come to their rescue before they make a bad decision.

They must rest assured that author Geary Reid has heard their cries and provided this simple, but important book, which will assist them in walking away from their problems. Geary Reid has problems like many other persons. He is not a superhuman. He has seen many persons struggle with their problems, and when some of them were unable to find proper and timely answers, they made bad decisions.

He is now saying that there must be an end to such bad decisions. People need to stay alive and not commit suicide. While life has problems, your problems are not greater than anyone else's problems. So, this book is important to help you to say yes to life and no to suicide.

Geary Reid feels hurt when persons take their lives. He knows that each person has great potential. He loves interacting with people and knows that when a person takes their life, he has lost a potential friend to talk with.

His passion for people goes beyond those who live within his community and country. As he listens to the news worldwide and learns of another person committing suicide, he often questions himself as to what he could have done to save that person. Because he cannot reach everyone, he wrote this book to help those persons who are alive and have problems. He wants to tell them all that they are not alone, since he had many problems but never gave up. He shared his problems with others, and they have assisted him to make good decisions.

He encourages persons to read this book today to stay alive. If you know someone who is going through many problems, purchase this book and present it to them so that they will stay alive. Ask them regularly if they have read this book, since it provides many life lessons to help persons to overcome their problems.

Life has many obstacles, but persons can overcome it. You are not the only person with problems. Live your today, expecting that tomorrow will be great. Do not give up on today, as greatness lies ahead of you.

Geary Reid sends his congratulations to everyone who has overcome. He challenges you to go and assist others to stay alive, just like you did.

www.ingramcontent.com/pod-product-compliance
Lightning Source LLC
Chambersburg PA
CBHW061253140726
47998CB00006B/2207